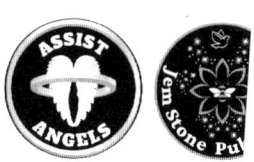

BROKEN

CHALLENGING AND COMIC POETRY

An Anthology of selected poems about unusual, unorthodox vignettes on life

Written by

PHIL HILL

Jem Stone Publications

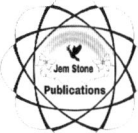

CONTENTS

A Tragic Life	5
Brief Encounter	9
The Law Of The Real-time Bus Screen	12
Variations On A Parenting Theme By Philip Larkin	14
Gospel According To The White Van Man	16
Stars Wars Prequel – The Return Of The Plastic Merchandising	19
If I Were Joyful	20
NAOMI	23
Uncle Phil	24
Great Grandpa's Campaign Medals	26
Dad's Memory Test	28
Poetry Salute To Captain Tom Moore	30
The End Of A Rainbow	32

CONTENTS

I AM KING	37
Lost?	41
Being TEN	46
Dear Iris	49
The Re-enactment Of The Last Supper - In An Asylum	51
The Road To Bedlam	53
Before Love	55
SORRY	58
My Molecule Encrustation	60
Despite Myself	62
I am on the Spectrum	65
Human Virus Receptacles	67
The Reluctant Hero	68

CONTENTS

I Am (A Frail Masculine Creed)	70
Downtrodden Generations	73
Which Emoji Are You?	74
A History Of Vegetables	76
On The Edge	79

A Tragic Life

You remember being disrespected
Talked down to
Ignored

Because you were a child
You were expendable

A small insignificant cog
In a machine
Controlled by your mother

You were a job to be ticked off the list
A person who should be quiet
Not messy

An inconvenient burden
You felt undeserved
Unloved

But to others
You were a dutiful wife

The committed sister
Doting aunt

Rebellious Daughter
And controlling mother

Some didn't like you
But I did care
And cared enough
To love you

Despite our differences
Others understood
Perhaps as much as you
How you were victim
And perpetrator of oppression

The hardship, the pain
The patriarchal control
That meant as a child and adult
You never felt free

A life-time of grudging sub-service
Unconditional love given
On restricted terms

How did you cope?

Trapped and in pain
In the kitchen-like prison
You were burnt out
With nothing to figure out

To you
Life was just a task
To be ticked off and completed

Few were the cases
When you could be really you

Always on duty
Unable to live in the moment

Those that knew you
Understood the sacrifice

The pain

A life given in service
And in duty

Brief Encounter

Women in uniform
Turn me on
Like the lady
Behind the Pharmaceutical Counter
And as I
Approached
Awkward questions
Emerged
About physical exertion
And pain control
When these questions were posed
The Red-headed lady
Peddled me a choice
The anti-inflammatory gel
Or the older men's nuclear option
'Voltarol'
I pondered staring
Into her pensive eyes

And then I peddled her
With my inadequate story
Of mid-life crisis, middle-aged
Hobbies under the umbrella
Topic 'Jogging'
And as I develop my over-familiar
Chat up
With my overweight beginnings
I conclude that my 14 stone
Carried by small feet
Would cause the inevitable foot pain
And testing whether she was
Hanging on my every word
I told her about my chocolate 5km race
'I finished third'
I boasted
But 'was beaten
By a twelve -year-old and
A woman dressed as a tooth fairy'
Emphatic laughter erupted from her

As she held the pain-killing gel
In her hand
And from then on
There were no awkward silences
At my local chemist
Particularly for the lady
In the blue and white uniform

The Law of the Real-Time Bus Screen

You know when
Yes when
When your bus is due
Then disappears from the screen
How would Einstein explain
That I mean
The sudden non-existence of buses
That is
Could it be
That the bus
Ceases to exist
And thereby breaks
The Newtonian Law
About the indestructibility of matter?
Or is it that
It has merely disappeared

Down a black-hole
At the bus terminus?
Or is it more likely
The driver has merely switched off
The satellite tracking mechanism
To knock off early?
And in the word of The Carpenter's song
Why do buses suddenly appear
Every-time the bus inspector
Draws near?
So, in the law of real-time bus screens
Buses can be suddenly created
And destroyed

So much for Newton
So much for Einstein

Variations on a Parenting Theme
By Philip Larkin

They fuck you up
Wrote Larkin
They don't mean to
But they do
He asserted
So, being fucked up
Is normal,
Excusable, legitimate?
But they do
The fucked-up bit I mean
Is an inheritance for all?
Parent's imperfections passed on
Like a politician who kicks the can
Down the road
But is it being fucked up
That counts?

Or is it
What you do with it
That counts?
Some parents inflict damage
By merely conducting their brokenness
Down a copper-like wire
Others contain their brokenness
Transforming themselves
To protect others
Including their off-spring
Leaving the remaining imperfections
Passed on in the usual way
So, their children are less fucked up

Gospel According To The White Van Man

White van man is to be found
Across the land
As many as grains
On a beach of sand
'Did you hear?'
'Did you hear?'
A white-van man said
As the blood of anger
Rushed to his head
He stood, a big-built figure
With coffee stains on his newspaper
The belt he wears holds it in
That face had long since lost its grin
'They come here'
'They come here'
'Get council house, NHS

Benefits the lot'
'That's a pretty damn sight
More than I've got'
'You pay your taxes
Rent for all those years
Working all hours, god sends
It's enough to drive you round the bend'
Paper in hand, unfurled
He puffs and grinds and reads
From the sixty-font print
As if from the pulpit
You couldn't make up this shit
Context irrelevant
The case-study that proves the rule
He will tell you he's nobody's fool
Then, he and his apprentice
Trade more facts
The HR Managers had better
Not catch them in the act
Tabloid statements from on high

The drivers think
They're modern types of guy
Bring back hanging or even the birch
And resurrect the stop and search
Across the country
White-van men
Seek to serve
The country gets the government
It deserves

Stars Wars Prequel – The Return of the Plastic Merchandising

Luke Skywalker is alive!!
Or, at least the plastic version is
And yes
He's swimming with dolphins
In the Pacific
He'd really made it now
From the last vestige of land-fill
Through the sewers
He was living the high-life
At least until he got swallowed
And now, he's wrecking
The internal universe
Of some marine creature
Showing on a BBC screen near you
Or on iPlayer

If I were Joyful

If I were truly joyful
I would smile
In my reflected face of fear
I would dance
In the rain
In spite of the on-lookers
I would perceive the sternest test
As an opportunity to shine
In front of my critics
I would dare to shout hallelujah
On Halloween
To make a cup of tea
For a sworn enemy at work
I would ask a flustered pensioner
At a checkout
To take their time
As a pre-emptive strike
For other random utterances of kindness

I would do lots of things
If I were truly Joyful
Regardless of the unmet need
For Caffeine
The cash-point being empty
The Bus - missing my stop
Full of passengers
My trip up on the snow
My Ownership of issues at work
Yes, I would do this
If the anchor of joy
Was truly secured in my heart
To stop me being buffeted
By the winds of change
Ignorance and ill-fortune
If the anchor of joy was secure
Things could get really bad
And I would believe
No matter how long it took
That transformation

Would take hold
And the seeds of good fortune
Would shoot up
From tragedy
Whether or not
I was used as an instrument
Of change
Or merely the location
Of divine intervention
True-joy is like a feeling
That blows like a candle
That the darkness
Can't put out

NAOMI

There were two Naomi's
A Barista and barrister
So, don't pick the wrong person
Otherwise, you end up in court
Offering the defendant, a coffee
As a line of defence
Or to be told how to plead
At the coffee house

Uncle Phil

He's always been ill in the head
His odours we dread
A face that for years
Was mask-like and drawn
Then with medication changes overdue
He had a reserved awkward-stare
Now!
It's as though he hasn't got a care
He's a decent bloke
With one-liner jokes
An agony uncle to all
When it comes to football
He knows the score
And when he philosophises
It's over your head
Just like the bad joke
That you can't get out of your head
I wouldn't say he's over qualified

But, with the letters after his name
He makes lesser-mortals terrified
The eternal student
He studied while it was prudent
Then he was now told
We've run out of courses
Back to the rat-race
His interviews were ace
His new medication
Getting him attention to details
He now knows what his job entails
The knock-on the door
Said that Uncle Phil has arrived
Chancing to stay for coffee
Until a meal by his sister is contrived

Great Grandpa's Campaign Medals

You're only
'Someone in the Army'
Great Grandpa said
So, he joined up
To get ahead
Born in Aston of Brummie-stock
An Empire to defend
To uphold himself no-end
General Kitchener
Assigned and conscripted
Liberation of Gordon in Khartoum
He enlisted in vain
For poor Gordon was slain
But the Sudanese were defeated
Campaign medal with glee he greeted
The Dutch settlers in South Africa
Took hold and rebelled
Another campaign to unfold

Ladysmith medal to uphold
Kitchener's poster-finger beckoning
He enlisted
Lying about his age and health
Emboldened
To the Army enlisted
Others were conscripted
Saying, 'You're a nobody
Unless you join the army'
'Then, you're a somebody'
In the trenches he fought
Another campaign medal he sought
Britain alone after Dunkirk
Again, he enlisted
But was turned back and resisted
'Hop it mate, and join the home-guard'
They said
An honorary campaign medal instead

Dad's Memory Test

Father ruler
Boy in hand
Players on wall
Brummie land
'At the back'
Coombes, Robson, Ross
Aiken and Nicholl
The boy recited
He got them all right
So, they were both delighted
At the front
The ruler went
'Graydon, Rioch and Little
'And that man in the tracksuit dad'
'Manager son'
He retorted
'Crowe', he got his first name distorted
In the middle, the ruler jabbed

'Not a clue, son'
The boy's thoughts
Pausing for a while
His thinking frozen
The mid-field not chosen
Anderson !, Hamilton !
And Godfrey, son
Remember the names
Don't be scared
And next time
Be better prepared

Poetry Salute to Captain Tom Moore

You were the change
We wanted to see
In ourselves
A more constructive way to be
Millions left clamouring
As the virus gave
Our lives a hammering
Isolated, distant, separated, withdrawn
You gave us hope
As we approach a new norm
Medals emblazoned
Dignity intact
Your image on TV
Gave us a point of contact
Firm your grip
On the wheeled walking-frame
We no longer felt the strain
As lap by lap

You took us back
To a time like when in time of war
Our freedoms are now
Threatened once more
You left behind a beacon of hope
Shone to those
Who had struggled to cope

The End of a Rainbow

A small gate
Lay open
On the horizon
Beyond which
The sun
Rose like a new dawn
Venturing forward
The path narrowed
Approaching the gate
The path fell away
At both sides
Leaving a jutting ridge
The path had been wider

BROKEN
CHALLENGING AND COMIC POETRY

From far out
But as the walk progressed
It had converged
Not only this
But what remained
Was a poor excuse
For what had been a road
Which wound one way
Then the other
But
Always
Always the gate
Remained in sight
Finally reaching my goal

BROKEN
CHALLENGING AND COMIC POETRY

I walked through
The light intensified
My companion
Seemed to glow so brightly
In a way that was beyond words
I could smell the fragrance of flowers
Never before encountered
At the same time
It seemed
Overwhelming
And elevated in mood
There was a sudden realization
An awareness of peace
Forgiveness and love intermingled

BROKEN
CHALLENGING AND COMIC POETRY

The clouds, which had hovered, lifted
In front of me was a panoramic view
I noticed the scenes
Of all that had gone before, in a flash
Below, I could see
The hospital bed
And loved ones crying
Hugging each other
Then the coffin
After which, I began to realize
The seeds I had sown
Had grown
Nieces and nephews got married
Starting new careers

BROKEN
CHALLENGING AND COMIC POETRY

Living on in lives
Of those I had touched
Then the crowds
Waiting
Of everyone I had ever met
Smiling, shaking hands
One at a time
For all the years of searching
I had finally arrived

I AM KING

I am a King – The Alternative Kingdom by Phil Hill

I am a King
But my Kingdom is not of this world
If it was
I would not have been betrayed by a kiss
Questioned by the community leaders
Brought to the authorities for judgment and punishment
In my Kingdom
People would have remembered
The people I healed
The outcasts I restored
The dead person I raised
They would have seen it
As an outward sign of a King
Exerting his power
Not to challenge the authorities
Of those who lead our community
But in their Kingdom

BROKEN
CHALLENGING AND COMIC POETRY

They look for another King
At the head of a liberating army
To upload the laws and the commandments
That had been handed down
To continue burnt offerings
Purchased from the money
Changes in the temple
My Kingdom is not of this world
If it was
The lion would lie with the lamb
People would love themselves and others equally
Because they all were loved first by me
Not liberating by governing lands
And wealthy plunder
But liberating hearts and minds
With the truth
Of love, of forgiveness, of realness
With themselves and others
In my Kingdom
Hope would spring a well of water

BROKEN
CHALLENGING AND COMIC POETRY

Endless by replenishing
In my Kingdom
Guilt would be banished by forgiveness
And from forgiveness would spring love
And it's fruits
In an abundant harvest
In my kingdom, everyone is called by name
And loved first by being themselves
So that they can love themselves
And shine that love to others
If my Kingdom were of this world
I would bound up the broken people
With the glue of love
Would seep into the cracks
So that they feel whole and healed
In my Kingdom
I would tend my people
Like a shepherd herds sheep
Those that stray would be yearned for
And called by name

And welcomed back into the fold
But my Kingdom is not of this world
But I am still King
A Servant King with a message of salvation
A King that would lay down his life
So, his message
His mission would live on
A message of hope
And a return to his followers
When his tombstone rolled away

LOST?

I lost thirty years
Holding out for love
Holding out that olive branch
Held out for that friendship

Holding out because the road travelled
Was too far
Held out because I thought
I could transform

The impression I had created
Holding out because it is my default setting
Feeling I was nothing without her
Her approval

Her love
Her way
Her truth

Her perception of me

As a misfit
As a loner
As the pursuer
Of love

Of acceptance
Of reconciliation
To repair all that had passed
Forgiven

Wiped clean
Twelve thousand miles of separation
That says no
You will evermore be

A misfit, loner, pursuer

BROKEN
CHALLENGING AND COMIC POETRY

I lost thirty years
Over the right fish
In the wrong pond

In the wrong decade
Thirty years lost
And 180 degrees of separation
Nothing to bridge the continents

The heart
The restless soul
I was always and evermore
Out of my depth

Fishing in the wrong pond
At the wrong time
In the wrong crowd
All that, mental recovery

BROKEN
CHALLENGING AND COMIC POETRY

Status, education
And wisdom
Wasted
I lost thirty years

Projecting into an abyss
Thirty years of hurt
My heart still bloody, still bleeding
But all singing and dancing

Her tune
Her voice
Her way

Until… Until the day
Discovery. Yes. Discovery
That "conditionality" was
The trap

BROKEN
CHALLENGING AND COMIC POETRY

Of wanting
Something in return
For something
I could still strive, climb, build

Expecting nothing in return
And let fate and supreme being
Surprise me
Forgetting what I had given

Sacrificed
Striven, pursued
And stood out far
Expecting nothing

Nothing
But surprised
By the ends that resulted
From the means
That took thirty years
To unfold

BROKEN
CHALLENGING AND COMIC POETRY

BEING TEN

The photo of you - Holte End

The backdrop
Claret and blue uniform

Nervous smile
And hands held pensively

You marched on the pitch
First team player in hand

How did you cope
With all that noise?

But you always conform
Particularly at school

Regardless of the struggle
Inside

And that release
The meltdown

BROKEN
CHALLENGING AND COMIC POETRY

Amongst the safety and security
Of those you love

When you can be honest

You can't fight or flee
You just freeze
Time stops still

But

As you give the thumbs up
In your new birthday tracksuit top

And every day that passes

You open up the narrow door
On your world

You put yourself into the world
Ot those you love

As the words and phrases
Of your emotional dictionary grows

That picture of the mascot
Is still on that bookshelf top

You're taller, older and wiser now
And what's more

You're ten

DEAR IRIS

We didn't relate
During those bonding years
Yet after more than a decade
Our eyes met
But didn't connect

I was puzzled
You cried non-stop
Your hair was grey
And your face and demeanor
Zapped of energy

Less than a decade later
A connection was made
And this time
I understood
From my own experience

Why you seemed
So empty and comatose
An empty shell
Now, it was my face
That was zapped

BROKEN
CHALLENGING AND COMIC POETRY

With a tired look, life had broken us both
Our nerves had been shattered
By unfulfilled love

The Re-Enactment of the Last Supper – In an Asylum

Dedicated to reverend Bob Gleeson

A quiet chaos broke out
At a routine communion
Quiet murmuring and unrest present
The offered hands
For the bread were shaking
The priest had earlier
Recited the liturgy
The wheel-chair maneuvered
Amongst the offered hands
And it's incumbent looked
And spoke at those receiving
Amongst the recipients
Some couldn't handle the bread
Some couldn't handle the wine
Many among the offered hands were

BROKEN
CHALLENGING AND COMIC POETRY

Confused, anxious, foreboding
Until the voice from the wheelchair spoke
Then calmness broke out
Many would return
To their local parishes
As well as the medication would allow
And they would quietly remember
The reverend who had been there
In their darkest moments

Each Sunday, the Asylum Chapel
The sound of tuneless hymns rang out
Accompanied by bodily smells
But the priest didn't care
These were God's chosen
Broken people
Among the chosen
Don't wear masks
Exposing their self-
Incriminating vulnerability

Broken people sharing the bread
The wine

Of mutual acceptance
And reciprocity

The Road to Bedlam

I walk into the early dawn
Down familiar roads
But the signs, the destinations
Are changed in my head
I remind myself I have awoken
And this is not a dreamscape
My surroundings familiar
Remembered in the light
And quietness of the early hour
Tormented and searching
For the person in my head
Absent, yet seemingly
Consciously present
For so long, a hold on my thoughts
But, outside my thoughts
My faulty thinking is absent in logic
The woman who fixates me
May not be into me
She may not want the attention

But still
She holds my thoughts
In her iron grip
From which I can but don't release
I can't access her world, her thinking
Though I think I can
And I walk down a familiar road
In search for her inviting thoughts
Thoughts of someone I think I know

And she seems to speak to me
While familiar people comment
But she's out of my reach
And has always been beyond me
And I arrive where she once lived
And realizing
This could be a cul-de-sac
A dead-end
I reach out a hand for help
To exit this psychotic world
In an ambulance

BEFORE LOVE

In the beginning
I was a formless brain
That walked on sticks
An island in a world that orbited me
Few were the connections to others
Many were the opportunities

To brag
To know more
To show more

In my own 'show me' show
Life was a competition
To be faster, smarter and better
But my outer skin was fragile
Buffeted by the winds of humiliation
And conditional regard

BROKEN
CHALLENGING AND COMIC POETRY

Love was a goal
Always a step away

A race away
An exam away
A job away

And how he could beat himself up

At the slightest set-back
Or parental disapproval

But, in truth, love was distant

A difficult leap to make
An encounter seemingly far away
Not understanding
Not perceiving
Oscillating between the ego-centric
And, self-loathing

Thought Cycles
I didn't get that someone
Would one day love
My silliness
My puns
My appearance

Or, would take pleasure
In ironing my shirts
Or, would ask me out
To the local church
Or, would want to spend
The lone waking hours
In my company

And yes, I didn't need to be
The smartest person

The fastest athlete
The richest person
I just needed to be me

SORRY

If
I make you feel
Awkward

If
You feel
Pressured

If
You squirm
At my unwanted advances

If
I don't really get
What you are trying to say

I am also
Awkward
Pressured
Shy

BROKEN
CHALLENGING AND COMIC POETRY

And don't understand
What I'm trying to say

Trying to make conversation
But going too deep
Making myself vulnerable
Small and meek

But don't take offense
The fault is mine
You are still beautiful and kind

I don't understand

And sometimes don't try

Perhaps I won't have to re-learn again
The lesson of unrequited love

My Molecule Encrustation

In the end
'All things must pass'
A famous Beatle once wrote
But when I pass
When my generation dies out
When every person
With a living memory of me
Is no more
What evidence will there be?
That I ever
Stood
Sat
Wept
Laughed
Will there be a lasting ripple?
In the space, time, continuum
The fragment of a poem I wrote
In a time-capsule

BROKEN
CHALLENGING AND COMIC POETRY

Viewed by another alien-being
Or
Will death be a new beginning?
To a different stream of consciousness
And, in the end
Does my stand-point
Derived from my own experience
Survive or prevail?
In the end
Is there a judgement?
A reckoning?
And yes
In the end
Am I more than a functioning set of molecule encrustations?
And does it really matter in the end?
I mean

Despite Myself

I am

Broken
Weak

Searching
By the grace of God

Yes, I am

I am

Doubting
Self-loathing
Searching

For the grace of God

BROKEN
CHALLENGING AND COMIC POETRY

Yes, I am

I am

Over-analysing
Over-thinking
Searching

For the grace of God

That is always present

Yet

I am

Tall
Strong
Intelligent and wise

BROKEN
CHALLENGING AND COMIC POETRY

By the grace of God

I am
I am

Enough
Sufficient
Prevailing

By the grace of God

I am
I am

What I am
Because of myself
Despite myself

Becoming myself

By the grace of God

 I am

I am on the Spectrum

An autistic man said
Pre-occupied with what
He says is going wrong in his head
Slapped and told he is
Stupid as a kid
The hectoring voice
Of his mother
From which he hid
Unable to forgive the
Occasional faux-pars
Trying to find self-harm
From sharp objects
In a jar
You're not a freak
The therapist said
His patience, self-doubt
Had filled up his head

BROKEN
CHALLENGING AND COMIC POETRY

You are different in
A gifted way
You just experience
The world
Differently each day
The neuro-typical takes
Their senses for granted
As a neuro-a-typical manages
Their life
So, their senses don't become
Over-heated
Usually you ask
What's wrong with me?
More unusual to say
You're ok
Just a different way to be
I have a name
And it's not in a diagnostic manual
I am a different type
Of human animal

BROKEN
CHALLENGING AND COMIC POETRY

Human Virus Receptacles

I am a human virus receptacle now
To be turned away from the shop door
Stadium and Pub
I am the human virus receptacle spreader
Until proved negative by lateral flow
I am human
And want to connect with others
Human virus receptacles
I was born this way
A tactile sexual-being
But, I am now turned away
From a kiss, a hug and embrace
We reject each other
Such is the pain, yearning
And disconnect

The Reluctant Hero

Grandad didn't talk
About the war
He didn't want to fight
He didn't like remembrance
He didn't wrap himself
In the flag
But, he hated Hitler
Yet, hated killing
Humans too
But one day, he
Couldn't hold back
And told my mother
About how he had killed a tall blond boy
In a German uniform and helmet
He remembered
The trauma
The hesitation
The revulsion

Before he put the bayonet in
He didn't want to kill
Least of all a probable Hitler Youth Graduate
But, he disliked the idea of dying himself, less
After that, the killing was routine
He just remembered how he killed his first boy
Other than that
Grandad never talked
A sole utterance to my mother
When he killed that tall boy
On that battle field
Grandad didn't like remembrance
He didn't wrap himself
In the flag
He just regretted having to kill
A tall blond boy in uniform
To save himself

I AM (A Frail Masculine Creed)

I am a scared man
Driven by the aversion to failure
Fine-tuning my learning in the only job I can still do
Scared of failure, mistakes, forgetfulness and blunders
I am a scared Christian
Driven by an internal need to like Jesus
Hoping for the way, the truth and the life
Fulfils in the long-game of life
I am a masculine oppressor
Driven by ego and an instinct to be liked
Failing to acknowledge my strengths
Where people like me have been traditionally controlling
And verbally abusive
I am a man and available in a world
Of relationship - committed women
Desperate to avoid a look or a stare
That could be viewed as intrusive
I am a Mental Health Survivor

BROKEN
CHALLENGING AND COMIC POETRY

Of an OCD-diagnosed controlling mother
And the unresolved trauma
That shapes my history
I am a paranoid being, labelled, conditioned to be scared
Insecure and anxious
Perceived as other than human
I am a white-male Christian and survivor
I look to a supernatural God
To give me an unconditional love
From which I can then love others more fully
I strive to forgive
So that I can avoid harsher judgment
Than I can handle
I own and learn from my mistakes
Hoping I don't have to re-learn from them
Yet, despite this long list
Of so-called male inadequacy
I'm enough
And I continue to prevail
Despite the insecurities, diagnosis

BROKEN
CHALLENGING AND COMIC POETRY

Stereotypes and misunderstandings
I am empowered by embracing
My relative powerlessness
In a world in which I negotiate
Reason and justify
To build up others
To share, not to hog the lime-light
To apologise and own when I am oppressive
To gain the most from the few remaining
Encounters in my life

Downtrodden Generations

When you look back
You realise, you see, you observe
The damage done
The way you trod down
And down on your dearest, so hard
They didn't spring back up like they had for so long
Like resilient children do
They developed a paranoia, insecurity and instability
That merge yours
The way you had been trodden on
And on and so on
Down the generations
No-one stopped this madness
They just passed it on
Everyone a victim - Everyone an oppressor
Yes, no-one had processed the pain
They just passed it on and on and on

Which Emoji Are You?

Is real happiness reflected
In a smiling yellow face?
Especially when short-term setbacks
Lead to long-term blessings
Enabling you to reflect that
Everything happens for a reason
Is a frown merely worn in jest?
To impress in a flirting ritual
Is the up-turned mouth of sadness
Really a bitter-sweet moment
When you realise the happy memories that go with grief
Isn't human-emotion and feeling
More complex than a singular expression
And what about those who don't wear their emotions
The good-old poker-faced card-players
Or smiling back-stabbers
Isn't the day we can modify human-feelings
Or put them in an emoji tock-box – snap-shot

The day we lose our real humanity
The day we turn fake
The day we deny true reflections on feelings that can change
And what about those who deceive with their expressions
They no longer have to act
They just press on a yellow-face to lie
Appearances, faking it and lies
Attract some who can take advantage of genuine emojis
Fake or real?
Which emoji are you?

A History of Vegetables

As praised by Casey Bailey, Birmingham Poet – Laureate.
'You give a voice to those who need to be heard'.

The brain saturated
The suppressants that kick in
From each tablet
Slow, his thoughts
He had not been able to
Handle them
Their speed, their intensity
He had presented to the world
Incomprehensible
But, he knew his
Thoughts and their painful logic
Intermingled, anxiety, depression and psychosis
With a painful, non-sensical narrative
But, a narrative understood by him
By the time the tablets had tamed the thoughts

Their intensity, their speed
He had come to a stand-still
As he would drift-off in sentence whilst talking
So thick the thoughts
And their logic
Couldn't connect together
Submerged in a fog
The retreat of self
A self that couldn't fill the void
Submerged, silent, regressing
As the months and weeks went by
How bright he had been
How infantile he had become
Because he couldn't handle
A crisis, during a short-period of his life
The label applied
The tablets supplied
The massive weight-gain
The vacant void
As you stared into his eyes

BROKEN
CHALLENGING AND COMIC POETRY

A voice that drooled in a pathetic whine
Medication reviewed, renewed
As they sanction a social-death
As they sanction another living-vegetable
To the scrap-heap

ON THE EDGE

The edge over which I fall
Surrender and give-up
On forgiveness, reconciliation, healing and wholeness
I am ok on the edge
It keeps me rooted, focus-driven
A slip, a momentary lapse
Can engender feelings of guilt
By association
And reputation
Spoiling the view on himself of himself
Living in bubbles
Shield the truth
Bubbles created by kindness and consideration
But bubbles don't protect, shield or deflect
They obscure, distort and delay
Until the moment of realisation
An epiphany
When I am sitting

BROKEN
CHALLENGING AND COMIC POETRY

On the edge
Over which I fall
Surrender and give up
But when and if I fall
There is a finality
That repels me
Sometimes yes, sometimes
I have travelled too far
To stop, to fall, to give up
Instead, the tension, the pain is endured
Knowing or more, hoping
The intensity will ease
Be processed
Worn, sanitised or can he hold the tension long enough
For the opportunity, yes
The opportunity
To co-exist
Be transformed
By the awareness
Being aware enough to feel as new creation

BROKEN
CHALLENGING AND COMIC POETRY

And stand-point
Revisiting temptations
To dis-own the 'me' that has a partial view
Perhaps with breaking out of the bubble
My gaze, my projection
Would leave others, able to continue
But the edge is still there
Created by
Conditioned by
The traumas, the paranoia, the insecurity or failure
I need to feel that I am sufficient
To be renewed
To feel a new creation
Whilst dis-owning the embodiment of me
That travelled so far to get there
To live life on the edge
Is a better place to be, for me?